SMART CONTRACTS IN BLOCKCHAIN

Table of Contents

Introducing Smart Contracts

Understanding Blockchain Technology

How Blockchain Is Changing the Financial Market

How Smart Contracts Affect Everyday Life

Ethereum: A Programmable Blockchain for Smart Contracts

Using Solidity to Build Ethereum Smart Contract

The Future of Smart Legal Contracts

To my parents

Introducing Smart Contracts

One of the most special features of blockchain is decentralization—that is, it is capable of being shared among all entities of the blockchain network, so removing the participation of third-party intermediaries or middlemen or third party. This feature is principally beneficial because it keeps you from the likelihoods of any process conflict while it is timesaving as well. While the blockchain technology is not perfect in their entirety, they provide quicker, inexpensive and more effective opportunities in comparison to traditional banking systems. Owing to this fact, even governmental organizations and corporate financial institutions are now shifting to blockchain.

Recently, the most used application of the blockchain technology is something called "smart contracts." Conceptualized by cryptographer and legal scholar Nick Szabo, the idea of a smart contract was born in 1994. Szabo concluded that any decentralized ledger could be used as smart contracts, which means these contracts will be self-executable and digital. By converting these digital contracts into code, they could then be executed on a blockchain.

While the concept of smart contracts had been around more than two decades ago, our present-day system functions on paper-based contracts. At times when digital contracts even come into play, they will still involve a trusted third party, which is very essential. And although we have managed to work out the rules and regulations of paper-based contracts, their effectiveness and smoothness cannot be relied on. If a third party is involved in any contract, the transactional fee is increased; in fact, the risk of fraudulent activities or securities problems increases as well.

So as blockchain takes foot in the digital technology landscape, these issues can now be effectively addressed. A blockchain-based system permits all the parties in the network to relate with each other in a distributed way, therefore removing the obligation of trusted third parties.

Simply put: blockchain is a technology capable of storing data on a distributed ledger. This stored data of transactions and records is available, in real-time, to all the entities in the network. As Bitcoin, the leading and most recognized form of cryptocurrency to date, became a buzzword in the digital work, blockchain technology started garnering the attention of mainstream media. Apart from its application in cryptocurrency, blockchain has advanced, spreading its seamless benefits across several industries.

Smart contracts are effective applications of the blockchain technology, and when used instead of traditional contracts they can lower the transaction costs considerably. The most well-known blockchain platform for the creation of smart contracts is called "Ethereum."

Developed in 2016, Ethereum is built on a feature known as "Turing-completeness"—which permits the creation of more custom-made smart contracts. From asset management to real estate to e-commerce to even smart homes, smart contracts are applicable across several fields and industries.

By definition, a smart contract is a computer code between two or more entities which is run on a blockchain technology, consisting of a set of fixed rules that are agreed upon by the participating entities. As the smart contract is executed, if these set of fixed rules are met, it will generate the needed output.

A smart contract is built on a computer code that permits decentralized automation, which facilitates, verifies and enforces the conditions of the principal agreement made by two or more parties. So if you want to exchange valuables, like property, shares or even money, smarts contracts will assist you in doing so transparently while removing the presence of a middleman (or third party), thus making the process free of conflict.

If we are to follow the traditional process of obtaining a court-registered document as a proof, we would have to first seek the services of a notary or an attorney, paying them for their services and waiting until the document is delivered. But with the rise of contracts, the status quo is changed totally. If we were to go the route of smart contracts, we would just obtain the necessary documents by simply paying for them without involving third parties, like notaries or attorneys. Furthermore, smart contracts are not restricted to simply outlining the rules around any agreement but are also in charge of implementing those obligations and rules automatically.

The vending machine analogy

A simple way of explaining smart contracts is by comparing the technology to a vending machine. Customarily, we would go to an attorney or a notary, pay them and wait to obtain the document. With smart contracts, we would just slip a Bitcoin into the vending machine (which stands as a ledger), and whatever needed document enters into our account. In fact, smart contracts not only outline the penalties and rules concerning an agreement (just like the traditional contract does) but also implement those responsibilities automatically.

Self-executable, self-verifiable and tamper-proof, smart contracts typically work on a system that comprises of digital assets with several parties; in the case, the involved entities can all oversee their assets. They can choose to either deposit these assets or redistribute among the other parties as stated to the obligation of the contract. Because of the lack of a third party and the ability to track the performance of assets on smart contracts in real-time, they are relatively cheaper and safer.

Real estate analogy

Another simple analogy for explaining smart contract is real estate business. For instance, say you have a property to sell—and the process of doing so requires several paperwork and hours of talks between several parties. Apart from the problem of communication, every contract will likely comprise the risk of fraudulent activities. In our present times, anybody willing to sell their home or apartment will do so by seeking the services of a real estate agent. These agents serve as middlemen in the entire process by working on negotiations and supervising the deal.

Since, in a situation like this, you cannot fully trust the other party you are selling to, the real estate agent would bring in the involvement of escrow services—they will be responsible for transferring the payment from one party to another party. Once the deal has reached finalization, you would need to make payments to both the real estate agents and the escrow services—in terms of commissions and percentages initially agreed upon. Therefore, in selling your property, you are losing more money and even taking more risks.

With the introduction of smart contracts, these issues can easily be worked out effectively. Blockchain-based smart contracts are made to function solely based on agreed-upon conditions. That is, the property can easily be passed over to the buyer once he or she has fulfilled the necessary conditions (payments and terms) that you have both agreed upon. So instead of depending on escrow services, a notable cheaper alternative is a smart contract.

In smart contracts, both the payment and the right of ownership are kept in a distributed ledger system, and the details are accessible in real-time to all the parties associated with the deal. By using a smart contract system, you will remove the need for a real estate agent or any third party for that matter. Of course, compared to your traditional options, you would be saving a significant amount of time and money with a digital contract.

Remember

As established, a smart contract is automatically responsible for the executing lines of code, which are stored on a blockchain network, and it is built around a set of rules made by the parties involved. If these rules are met, these codes are charged with executing autonomously and providing the output. Therefore, for business deals and collaborations, worked around agreed terms by two or more consenting parties, smart contracts play an important role. By converting contracts into computer code, this format allows for the code to be kept and replicated on the system—allowing it to be managed by a computer network that runs on blockchain. Whenever valuables (money or assets) are transferred and received on this network, a ledger feedback is available for all parties to see, thus ensuring transparency.

Understanding Blockchain Technology

Before we can go deep into the exciting world of smart contracts, we need to understand its foundation: blockchain technology. Our society is run by technology today. And with the rising demand for innovation in our everyday lives, more and more people are taking up new technology. From voice recognition software to augmented reality to artificial intelligent (AI) virtual assistants, this new technology is making our lives easier over the last decade. And with the acceptance of blockchain technology, the way we do is things are bound to get easier.

As established, a blockchain is a chain of blocks which contains information or data. In spite of being invented earlier, the first effective and widespread application of the blockchain technology began in 2009—by Satoshi Nakamoto. Using blockchain technology, he made the first digital cryptocurrency and termed it "Bitcoin."

Blockchain, an innovative technology that impacts several industries astonishingly, was first presented to the mainstream media when Bitcoin came into prominence. Bitcoin is simply a type of cryptocurrency (digital currency) that can make use of instead of officially sanctioned currency for transactions. And the principal technology which leads to the attainment of cryptocurrencies is blockchain.

There is a popular mistaken belief among people that blockchain and Bitcoin mean the same thing. But the truth is far from that. Making cryptocurrencies is just one of the many blockchain applications, and apart from Bitcoin, we have several other applications running on blockchain technology.

Simply put, blockchain is a global database which consists of transactional records; it is a data structure thus is secure, transparent and decentralized. Blockchain can also be expressed like a chain of records (kept in the form of blocks) that is supervised by not one distinct authority. In other words, it is a distributed ledger which is entirely open to every party on the network. When an information is kept on a blockchain, it is very hard (if not impossible) to alter or manipulate it.

Every blockchain-based transaction is protected with a digital signature which shows its legitimacy. Because of the use of digital signatures and encryption, the data kept on the blockchain is cannot be tampered with or altered.

Blockchain technology permits all the parties in a network to come to an agreement, generally called a "consensus." Every data deposited on a blockchain is digitally logged and has a shared history that is accessible by all the parties in the network. Due to this, the likelihood of duplicitous activities and falsified transactions is removed. Moreover, because of its decentralization feature, there is no need for a third party in every transaction.

For a simpler breakdown of how blockchain works, think about this instance: you are trying to send funds to someone who lives in another country and you are considering your options. The traditional way is to use either your bank or online payment transfer service such as PayPal. With all these conventional methods, a third party (local bank or PayPal) is required so as to help with the transaction. So, either as transfer charge or fee, additional cash is deducted by the third party. Apart from incurring additional charges in traditional cases, you cannot guarantee the safety of your cash as it is very likely that a cyber attacker might interrupt the network and take your hard-earned cash. Either way, the customer will eventually bear the brunt. Therefore, blockchain plays a vital role.

So rather than utilizing a local bank for cash transactions, we can instead use blockchain to escape the problems and risks of the traditional ways—a simpler and more secure form of banking. Likewise, no additional fee is needed because the money is processed by the participants directly, removing the involvement of a third party. And since decentralization is a major feature of the blockchain database, it is not restricted to any one location. This means that all the records and information are stored on the blockchain are decentralized and public. As the information is never deposited in one place, there is no likelihood of information being corrupted even by the best hackers.

How blockchain works

Information is stored on every block in the blockchain network, with each block containing the hash of its preceding block. By definition, a hash is an exclusive mathematical code belonging to a particular block. If the information within a block is altered, the block's hash will have to undergo alteration as well. Therefore, this linking of blocks via exclusive hash keys gives blockchain a strong protection.

Although transactions occur on a blockchain, we have designated network "nodes" responsible for validating each transaction. These nodes use the model of "proof-of-work" in processing and validating every transaction on the network. For a transaction to be validated, each block is required to correlate with the hash of the previous block. In this case, the transaction will only occur if the hash is accurate. If a cyber attacker tries to hack the network and alter information on any particular block, in this case the hash connected to the block will have to be subjected to modification as well. This breach can be easily discovered if the altered hash is not matching up with the other ones. This system guarantees that the blockchain is unchangeable because any alteration performed on the series of blocks will be mirrored through the whole network and, of course, will be easily discovered.

A breakdown of a blockchain transaction

- A blockchain network uses private or public keys so as create a digital signature that guarantees consent and security for every transaction.
- After authentication is done via these keys, authorization is also required.
- Blockchain permits parties of the network to do mathematical authentications and come to a consensus, therefore agreeing on any specific value.
- In the process of transferring something, the sender will make use of his or her private key, announcing the information of the transaction throughout the network. After this, a block is formed which contains information like the public key of the receiver, timestamp, and digital signature.
- This information block is then announced throughout the network, initiating the process of validation.
- To process this transaction, network-wide miners (people who create Bitcoins) begin to solve the mathematical problem linked to the transaction. For miners to solve this puzzle, they require computers with extremely high processing power and high electrical power usage.
- When a miner becomes the first to solve a puzzle, he or she is rewarded with Bitcoins—this process is called "mining." And this type of puzzle (mathematical problems) is called the proof-of-work
- Immediately most network nodes reach a consensus, agreeing to a mutual answer, the system timestamps the block and include it to the current blockchain. This block can comprise any information—from messages to data to even cash.
- Once the new block is linked to the blockchain, the older copies of the blockchain are kept up-to-date as well.

Features of blockchain

The following features keep the groundbreaking technology of blockchain unique:

1. Decentralized: Blockchains are totally decentralized. This means that nobody or group have absolute control of the entire network. Although every participant in the networks owns a replica of the distributed ledger, not one person is capable of modifying it alone. This exclusive feature of blockchain gives room for security and transparency while granting power to all parties—because everyone is equal.

2. Peer-to-peer network: Because of the way blockchain is set up, a peer-to-peer interaction between two parties is straightforwardly done without the need of middlemen. Blockchain makes use of P2P protocol that permits all parties in the network to own the same copy of transactions, allowing consent via a mechanized consensus. Take, for instance, if you want to perform a transaction in another country, you can use blockchain to do it quickly. Besides, any additional charges or interruptions will not be removed during the transfer process.

3. Immutability: The immutability feature of a blockchain means that data entered on the blockchain can never be altered or deleted. To comprehend immutability, consider the process of sending an email. When you send a broadcast email to 5,000 recipients, you cannot retract it. If you want to get rid of that email, you will need to tell every recipient to get rid of it, which is quite a wearisome process.

Therefore, immediately a data is processed on the blockchain, it can never be changed or altered. And even when you attempt to alter the data one bock, you will need to alter the whole blockchain, because each block keeps the hash of its previous block. An alteration in one hash will cause a modification in all the subsequent hashes. It is tremendously difficult for anyone to alter all the hashes because it demands a lot of computational power to perform this. Therefore, any data kept in a blockchain is immutable—free of cyberattacks or changes.

4. Cannot be tampered with: Because of the immutability feature fixed in blockchains, detecting the meddling of data is very easy. Tamper-proof and safe, any change (even in one block) in a blockchain will be easily spotted and tackled swiftly. To detect the meddling of data, the blocks and hashes are studied.

As we have established, each hash function (linked with a block) is exclusive to that block. It is more or less the "fingerprint" of that block. Any modification in the data will cause a modification in the hash function. And because one block's hash function is connected to that of the following block, if a cyber attacker is going to perform any alterations, he or she must have to alter the hashes of all the other blocks—this is extremely difficult for anyone to do.

Kinds of blockchains

While blockchain seemed to have advanced and spread into different works of life, there are basically two major types of blockchains classification: private blockchain and public blockchain.

Before we head toward the dissimilarity between these two, let us see the parallels between private blockchain and public blockchain:

- Both private and public blockchain have P2P networks that are decentralized
- All the parties in the network own an identical copy of the common ledger.
- Via a consensus, the network is responsible for maintaining the duplicates of the ledger as well as synchronizing the newest update.
- To prevent malicious attacks, the rules for safety and immutability of the ledger are agreed upon and used on the network.

Since we understand the similarities between these blockchains, let us explain their differences.

1. Public blockchain: This is a ledger that requires no permission, so it accessible by anybody at any time. As long as this person can access the Internet, he or she is authorized to obtain and access a public blockchain. Furthermore, anyone can as well see the entire blockchain history as well as make transactions via it. Public blockchains typically compensate the parties in their network for carrying out the process of mining and preserving the ledger's immutability. The Bitcoin is one prominent example of a public blockchain.

Public blockchains permit a global community of users to share information securely and freely. Nevertheless, a clear drawback is the possibility of being negatively affected if the agreed-upon rules are not implemented firmly. Besides, the rules agreed upon and applied at the outset have a very small scope of adjustment in the future stages.

2. Private Blockchain: They are exclusively shared among trusted parties. The entire supervision of the network is controlled by the owners. Also, the private blockchains rules can be altered, according to several factors such as authorization, members count, exposure and levels of permissions, and more.

Private blockchains can function self-sufficiently or can be assimilated into other blockchains too. These are typically utilized by organizations and enterprises. So, in private blockchains, trust level among the parties involves is higher.

Application of Blockchain

1. Cryptocurrencies: We can integrate blockchain technology into numerous areas. The main use of blockchains today is as a distributed ledger for cryptocurrencies, most particularly Bitcoin. A majority of cryptocurrencies utilize blockchain technology in recording transactions.

Although cryptocurrency was the first widespread application of blockchain technology, its importance has spread across several industries worldwide.

2. Smart contracts: Many private bodies and businesses interact with each other so as to exchange products or services. These transactions usually come with conditions and terms which have to be agreed upon by all participants—this can be in form of contracts or agreements. But the problem is that these paper-based contracts are susceptible to human hazards (fraud and errors), which tests the trust level between the parties involved, thereby raising the risk of doing business.

However, with blockchain-based smart contracts, these problems are be easily addressed. While smart contracts are capable of performing the same purposes as paper-driven contracts. The distinguishing feature around smart contracts is that they are digital and self-executable. By being self-executable, specific rules in the contract's code are deployed and executed automatically.

As we now know, blockchain-based smart contracts are planned contracts that can be completely or partly enforced or executed without human involvement. One of the key purposes of a smart contract is to automate escrow (a bond, deed or document kept in the custody of a third party and taking effect only when a particular condition has been met). Because smart contracts are based on blockchain technology, the chances of moral hazards are reduced and the use of general is optimized.

3. Banks: Most parts of the financial industry are applying distributed ledgers in banking at a fast rate. Because it is capable of speeding up back office settlement systems, banks are invested in this technology so as to improve the efficiency and lower costs of their financial services.

4. Other uses: Blockchain technology can be leveraged in creating a lasting, public, clear ledger system for collecting data on sales as well as monitoring digital usage and payments to content creators.

Remember

While many businesses are still reluctant to make blockchain the core of their business structure, the future of blockchain is bright. With the original concept of dependable records and transferring power to users' hand have massive potentials; blockchain-based smart contracts are bound to revolutionize the system. And with the introduction Ethereum, smart contracts have thrived in the blockchain ecosystem. Smart contracts can be used across an array of industries or situations—from financial agreements to crowdfunding to real estate property to even health insurances.

How Blockchain Is Changing the Financial Market

Since its inception in 2008, blockchain technology has played a major role in changing the way business is been done. While even in its early stages, this technology has managed to disrupt several sectors and industries. Its features, like transparency, immutability and decentralization, have made it quite attractive for business domains and sectors worldwide. One of such sectors that is making giant strides in harnessing the blockchain potential is the backing and finance sector.

Although there have been numerous challenges currently facing the rise of blockchain, it can certain agreed upon that it is capable of transforming the finance and banking sector by lowering service and labor costs. Across the globe, more and more financial executives are starting to reckon with blockchain technology. In addition, tech companies are always trying to leverage the system by spreading its application across other industries.

Because millions of dollars are constantly transferred from one part of the globe to another within 24 hours, the importance of blockchain is evident. Because the operation of our current banking and finance industry majorly relies on manual networks, the risk of human hazard (fraudulent activities and errors) is very high, which could result to a broken-down system of money management.

How it changes the banking sector

As we know understand the basic principle behind blockchain technology, the next phase is to see how blockchain can be used in the most efficient ways. We should also ask ourselves: is this technology going to become a fad or become a major aspect of our lives?

As predicted by many observers, blockchain will in years to come become to banks what the Internet has become to media. Financial organizations and banks will be using this technology to address most of their present-day challenges. It will become an alluring backbone of doing because it is more transparent, decentralized, secure and relatively low-cost, if compared to their existing system.

Whether it is the exchange of funds, information or data, the technology offers a very sophisticated and secure level of doing business. By providing the parties involved with a clear view of how their money is handled, trust is earned and business is done more smoothly.

In their bid to secure funds for customers, financial institutions require the services of many third parties. Because of the activities of these third parties, the cost of banking and transaction becomes more expensive. In fact, with too many individuals handling the processing and safekeeping of money, the probability of fraudulent activities and human error surges.

However, with blockchain technology, all the hard work will be done by the system automatically. Hence, transactions will become more secure and service cost will drop sharply. And most importantly, the overall customer experience improves significantly.

How some financial bodies are leveraging blockchain

While the financial world was very skeptical about blockchain technology in its infancy, the story seen a drastic change today.

As blockchain technology continues to thrive across several industries, financial bodies became among the first people in line to take advantage of its benefits.

Top financial brands such as JB Morgan Chase, a US multinational investment bank, have steadfastly embraced the blockchain system. By developing *Quorum*, an internal division specializing in the research and execution of blockchain technology, the bank has become a major player in this technology. Quorum is a smart contract and distributed ledger platform for organizations—it capable of supporting quick transactions and outputs, thereby tacking the major problems of the financial sector.

Another top bank in the US, Bank of America, has already a filed a patent document that discusses the execution of a permissioned blockchain to secure records and authenticate personal and business personal data. This system would permit only authorized parties in accessing the data as well as keeping logs of every logging entry. Furthermore, this planned system would use blockchain technology to join several in-use data storage system into a single body. This will produce a secured singular network that is capable of increasing the effectiveness and lowering the number of user data storage points

Goldman Sachs, another top finance player, is currently invested in researching and supporting a technology that is enables distributed registry. By creating *Circle*, a well-sponsored cryptocurrency venture that is bound to make big strides in the blockchain landscape, they plan to put an end to the major challenge of digital currency volatility. In so doing, they will make the financial industry more dependable with cryptocurrency options. And because Goldman Sachs aims to become the crypto kings of Wall Street, they are also in process of creating a branded cryptocurrency trading desk that specially handles its digital trades.

Blockchain application in finance

Here are a few ways the adoption of blockchain will change things in the financial sector over the coming years:

1. Reduce fraudulent activities: When it comes to matter matters, the chance of fraud is very likely. More especially for a system that operates on a basic cash model, security is very crucial. And due to the sophistication of economic crimes today, several financial institutions and third parties (such as stock exchange and money transfer service providers) are very liable to huge loses. This loss is caused by the dependence on a centralized database system used in managing funds and operating transactions. This system is highly susceptible to cyberattacks and system exploitation. For a stronger system to prevent such invasion and looting of hard-earned money, blockchain is a safer and tamper-proof technology that operates on a distributed database system. Because of the distributed feature of blockchain, the likelihood of system failure is close to nil. Because every transaction is kept in a block-based cryptographic form, it is very hard to corrupt the system.

In addition, each block in the system is connected to each other with a networking mechanism in such a way that if one a breach is found in one block, the other blocks will show the alteration in real-time. With this tracking feature, the breach can easily be noticed, thus giving the cyber attacker no room to alter the entire system. With the implementation of a safer blockchain system, cyberattacks and crimes, which plague the banking and finance industry today nowadays, will be significantly reduced.

2. Knowing your customer (KYC): By complying with the rules of Know Your Customer (KYC) and Anti-Money Laundering (AML), financial bodies are always overwhelmed when carrying out all these time-consuming processes. Millions of dollars in expenditure are used up to comply with these regulations annually, so as to prevent terrorist activities and money laundering. As a standard regulation, banks in the US have to upload their customers' KYC data to a central registry that can be used to check new or existing customer information. If blockchain is fully adopted in the system, the internal verification of each customer by a particular financial body or bank would be available to other institutions; therefore, the process of starting the KYC does not have to start all over again. Because of blockchain technology, time would not be wasted in duplicating customer data. In addition, every update to customer data in one bank will reflect in real-time across all other financial institutions. Due to this, administrative work and cost of compliance will be reduced across all departments.

3. The introduction of smart assets

Trade finance can become in actual fact perplexing if asset transactions needed to be logged with a specific timestamp and date. The fact is that global supply chains work with several components and entities that are being sold and purchased endlessly. And the paperwork needed in recording these details of supply and demand is even more complex. However, with the introduction of blockchain-based smart assets, records are stored in a digitized format and updated in real-time. A system running on a smart asset is not restricted to just recording how items from one point to another; it is also responsible for tracking the location of where items come from and where they are delivered.

4. The rise of smart contracts

Smart contract is the future of the financial industry; its application will be crucial in improving the banking processes and services. Because it improves the speed and simplifies intricate transaction processes, the ease of doing business is improved as well. Smart contracts will likewise guarantee that information exchanged during any transaction is valid—as approval is only possible when all the agreed-upon conditions of the smart contract code are fulfilled. So, if the rules and conditions are available to all the participants associated with the transaction, the likelihood of error during the period of implementation drops significantly.

5. Introduction of trade finance

In the backing industry, trade finance could well be one of the most important blockchain applications. With trade finance, participants associated with intricate bank transactions can be on boarded on a blockchain network; likewise, information can be exchanged among banks, importers, exporters on a shared distributed ledger. If the specific conditions of the agreement are fulfilled, a smart contract will, by design, implement them by itself—with all involved participants capable of viewing and accessing every action carried out. Using the blockchain technology, big names in the financial industry, like Barclays, have fruitfully implemented trade transactions which would typically take seven to ten days in just four hours. In comparison to current systems, blockchain technology will significantly lower the cost overhead charges such as the cost of ticketing and licensing.

How Smart Contracts Affect Everyday Life

The application of smart contracts to our everyday activities brings massive changes to the way business is done. Compared with traditional contracts, smart contracts are significantly faster and easier to execute, giving people and organizations the opportunity to properly reorganize their workflows. With valuables, such as cash or property, being exchanged, these contracts offer the right amount of security and convenience.

Moreover, because smart contracts are built on the blockchain technology, which is founded on openness, transparency is a key factor to these contracts. Every requirement, condition, or term of a transaction has to be checked, agreed upon and met by the involved participants, thus removing the likelihood of problems and disputes at the final stages of the terms and conditions. In fact, since the information is accessible to every party associated with the contract, the chances of miscommunication are lowered.

When drafting traditional contracts or documentation between two parties, the process takes could days, as several third parties would most likely be involved to slow down the process. However, smart contract works on software code, running with the speed of the internet. Transactions are completed at lightning speed, saving hours, unlike any regular business procedure.

With speed also comes accuracy. The code of a smart contract is clearly meticulous, requiring that all terms and conditions be met before it eventually executed. If a term or condition were not found in the contract, it would not be executed. Because of this fact, smart contracts beat traditional contracts in terms of precision and accuracy, as the chances of human error are lowered.

Safe and efficient, smart contracts function on an autonomous code, offering the most secure data encryption technology today. Meeting such top-quality safety measures, they are scalable in their reach, with thousands of transaction being executed without a glitch. As already established, the effectiveness of a contract is linked with its accessibility among all participants. Every information is stored on the blockchain network and can be accessed anytime.

There is also the cost-effectiveness factor when thinking smart contracts. Compared with regular contracts, parties do not have to involve or pay money to third parties or middlemen. No need to hire an attorney or even draft up a paper. Due to the fact that everything is coded, the paperless feature of smart contracts promotes convenience and seamlessness.

Finally, as a self-executing contract, the security, and openness feature of smart contracts encourage business trust and confidence. There is no room for manual alterations or human error. If all conditions are met, the contract executes itself automatically executes—reducing the need for courts, lawyers or litigation.

Smart contracts applications

Whether you are purchasing services or products or applying for a new job, contractual agreements come to serve as evidence of such actions. Nevertheless, the intricate processes of regular contracts and paperwork are expensive, involve intermediaries, and are prone to manual errors.

As technology and digitization advances, smart contracts will allow these processes to be faster, more effective, and inexpensive. When third parties and middlemen are eradicated, efficiency and effectiveness become the buzzword. Here is a list of sectors and industries that would benefit from this technology:

Insurance firms

Because of the absence of automation in insurance bodies, processing of claims take several months to execute. This could result in a huge dilemma for insurance agencies and their clients whom would be stuck in time constraints while trying to get their money. Likewise, agencies will have to deal with problems such as inefficiency, poor customer satisfaction, and unwelcome administrative costs.

When smart contracts are implemented in such processes, they would be simplified and streamlined, as payment for claims would be automatically triggered when terms and conditions are met based on the agreement of the agency and client. For instance, if there was a natural disaster that brings massive loss, smart contracts can be aptly executed in a way that clients can claim and use their funds in such difficult times. Any explicit information, such as the scope of loss inflicted, can be stored on the blockchain and the amount of reparation can be consequently decided.

Internet of Things

With the aid of sensors, the Internet of things (IoT) technology is being deployed to link commonplace devices to the internet so as to enhance system interconnectivity. These devices can as well be linked to the blockchain network to monitor all the processes and products in the system. For instance, in a common situation, consider the case of a customer shipped the wrong order after buying a product online with a paying system linked to IoT and blockchain. Because of these technologies, the customer would know beforehand by tracking the product's location and information (from its warehouse exit to transportation, shipment, and doorstep delivery). As the system is fully automated, product tracking becomes an effortless affair. This is possible because system sensors, working alongside smart contracts, can form their nodes on the blockchain—therefore the possession and location of any product can be tracked. The smart contract not only tracks the location status but also keeps updating it until the product is correctly delivered to the customer's front door.

Mortgage loans

A mortgage agreement is an intricate affair because many factors, such as outgoings, credit score and mortgage income, are involved. For a mortgage loan to be executed, it is very crucial that all these factors completely checked. Third parties and middlemen are known to handle this process, which is often drawn-out and worrisome for both the loan applicant and the lender. However, if smart contracts are leveraged in such cases, the benefits would be astounding, as third-party systems and intermediaries would be eradicated, removing the need for any drawn-out and worrisome process. In fact, relevant information is kept in a central location, which is available to all involved parties at all times.

1. Employment contracts: Smart contracts can also play an important role when drafting employment contracts. For traditional employment contracts, if the employee or employer does not meet up with the previously established conditions, there would be a breach in the terms of agreement. This could raise trust issues among the parties affected and even lead to more legal problems. However, with smart contracts, such issues can be addressed effectively. When both parties share a smart contract, the terms and conditions are explicit and fair for all to see and review. The information on these contracts could include job responsibility, salary amount, work durations, and so on. As soon as these transactions are logged on a smart contract, should any conflict arise, they can be easily accessed by the involved participants. This way, the employer-employee relationship is greatly fostered.

In addition, smart contracts can be leveraged to make the process of wage payment more effortless, as the relevant employee gets the agreed payment at the agreed time. Similarly, in the case of short-term employment, where the job candidate, employer and recruitment agency are concerned, smart contracts can be deployed to show openness. The contract is capable of preventing any recruitment agency from meddling with agreement terms of the candidate after being hired by the organization. With the help of smart contracts, any alterations made in the terms of agreement can be easily discovered by all parties involved.

2. Protecting copyrighted content. In today's digital landscape, the meaning of content can be very expansive. It could range from audio and video files to handwritten documents. Hypothetically, once a piece of content is commercially released, the content's owner gets a royalty fee. Nevertheless, creative processes often demand several participants; therefore, all involved members are legally likely to receive royalty or payments for their work. However, in reality, this is not usually the case, as entitlement conflict among people can result in lengthy litigations, as there is no well-defined technique of settling the problems of claims and entitlement. But with smart contracts, confusion about royalties can be easily resolved when the contribution of every party to the content is recorded on a blockchain network.

Thanks to the internet, digital content can easily be replicated and circulated. Because of this, any person from across the globe is capable of copying, replicating, and using it without giving credits to the legitimate owner of the content. While we have copyright laws to safeguard owners of intellectual properties, according to collective worldwide standards, these laws are not properly well explained. This means that a valid law in China might not legally acceptable in the US.

Even when there are copyright laws applied to intellectual contents, owners are quite prone to forfeit control over their data and encounter monetary losses. With the help of blockchain technology, copyrights can be kept in the form of smart contracts, thereby enabling business automation, increasing online sales, and removing the risk of redistribution. From creators of content to their consumers, a smart contract provides copyright clarity for everyone. Once a content owner registers his or her work on the blockchain network, they will have a tamper-proof evidence of their ownership. Moreover, because of the immutability feature of blockchain, every recorded entry on it can never be altered or deleted. The creator of the content will have complete control over content distribution and ownership.

3. Supply chain: Supply chain management requires the movement of products from the first stage to the last. As a core aspect of several companies, the appropriate operation of the supply chain is important to any business. Because a supply chain demands a line of workers to be effective, it is not a one-man job and so requires collaboration and some level of synchronization among workers. By leveraging smart contents in the supply chain, ownership rights of products can be recorded as they flow through the supply chain. Therefore, every worker in the network is capable of tracking the location of the goods at any point in time. At each stage of their transfer to the end customer, the product can be monitored throughout the process of delivery. If an item is misplaced during this delivery process, smart contract can be deployed to track it down. In addition, if any party does not meet up the conditions of the contract, it would be open for the entire network to detect, thereby ensuring transparency to the entire supply chain system.

Most times, supply chains are disadvantaged by paper-based systems. Before approval of any sort, forms have to pass through various channels, thereby increasing the risk of loss and fraud. The blockchain cancels out this by proving a secure and handy digital platform to all participants on the chain, where payments and tasks are automated.

When it comes to managing drug supply, for instance, smart contracts can be helpful when deployed in healthcare. Once a drug (of known name and amount) is set to be transferred from the manufacturer and to the pharmacist, a smart contract (stored with real data such as the supply quantity, drug information, etc.) can be deployed. Such a contract will be tasked with the management of entries throughout the length of the supply chain, monitoring every intermediate stop and channel.

4. The electoral process: While many professionals strongly claim that the voting system is very difficult to rig, but nevertheless, smart contracts would resolve any concerns by offering a significantly more secure system. First, to decode and access ledger-secure votes, which smart contracts would provide, attackers would have need massive computing powers, which nobody in the world possesses. Second, smart contracts would address the problem of low voter turnout, which is usually caused by the clumsy process of lining on queues, displaying identity, and filling forms. If smart contracts are introduced, online voting will be more secure, effective, and easy as voters cast their ballots en masse from the comfort of their homes.

No matter the level of security of the electoral process, criminal elements will still try to commit voter fraud. In addition, since our existing voting system functions on a manual process, the likelihood of manual errors is high. With smart contracts, however, the entire voting process can be automated, ensuring security and transparency of voters while upholding voter privacy and fair elections.

5. Business Management

Apart from the being a trusted single ledger, the blockchain network also enhances workflow and communication because it runs on an automated system that is transparent and accurate. Often, business operations are known to carry out many deliberations before a decision is made; they would also have to wait for approval before an external or internal issue can be addressed. However, if a blockchain ledger is used, the process can be streamlined, as it removes inconsistencies that usually happen with teams not working together. With such ledger, everyone will be in sync and the risk of expensive settlement delays or litigations is removed.

6. Identity management

As our society even becomes more digitalized, financial transactions have gone mostly online: we enter our details and security password so as to access our money. However, in such a situation, the identity of the person withdrawing or using the funds cannot be ensured, no matter how secure the bank is. Once the password and username of accounts are hacked, money is life unsecured. However, if there is a system capable of managing personal identification online, security is considerably increased. Thankfully, the distributed ledger technology of blockchain technology provides sophisticated ways of private-public encryption, on which users can verify their identity and digitize their documents.

This especially secure identity can be deployed when performing any transaction or interacting online on a mutual economy. In fact, this identity can help bridge the gap between several private and government organizations through blockchain-based general online identity solution.

Remember

While smarts contracts are still comparatively an emerging technology, they would soon spread like wildfire. From simple private agreements to government-sanctioned contracts, smart contracts will become a preferred alternative to traditional paper-based agreements. Both buyers and sellers will able to track purchases in the supply chain and encourage trustworthiness.

Looking at the expensive cost of running through attorneys and government agencies when drafting agreements, smart contracts provide an inexpensive method free of the third-party system. As long the code is checked, the execution of smart contracts is automated, offering the chance of more streamline routine processes and transactions. As technologies continue to evolve over the years to come, smart contracts will become widespread to come because of its obvious benefits.

Ethereum: A Programmable Blockchain for Smart Contracts

We already know the role blockchain plays in making verifiable and distributed transactions possible. One major instance of this is Bitcoin—the most well-known cryptocurrency in the world. Bitcoins, amounting to millions of dollars, makes it one of the most important examples of how the blockchain technology is very viable.

Ethereum, on the other hand, is the answer to this question: what would happen if application or service providers in the world vanished today? Ethereum is a platform capable of running decentralized applications—applications that do not depend on central servers.

A recap of the blockchain technology

A blockchain is data store that is verifiable and distributed. It functions by combining public key cryptography with the unique model of proof-of-work. Every transaction performed on the blockchain networked must be approved by the legitimate owner of the asset being traded. When new coins (assets) are formed, they are given to the owner. Sequentially, this owner is capable of preparing new transactions and sending those coins to other people by just inserting the public key of the new owner into the transaction, then approving the transaction with a personal private key. In doing so, a verifiable link of transactions is generated; each new transaction, as well as the new owner, will point to the preceding transaction, as well as the preceding owner. To manage these transactions and avoid the double-spending issues (duplicating or falsifying of coins), blockchain technology deploys the proof-of-work model.

The proof-of-work is a system that generates a cost for assigning transactions in a specific order and including them to the blockchain. These assignments of transactions are referred to as blocks. Each block is pointing to a preceding block in the chain, hence the term "blockchain." My ensuring blocks are expensive to create and ensuring each new blocks points to the preceding block, any potential hacker trying to change the history of transactions as shown in the blockchain has to pay the cost of each block changed. Since blocks link to preceding blocks, changing old blocks demands paying the cost for every block after it, therefore ensuring alteration to old blocks highly expensive. A blockchain raises the trouble of changing the blockchain by ensuring the cost of generating blocks is founded on a computational basis. Simply put: to generate new blocks, a specific amount of CPU power needs to be exhausted. Because CPU power relies on technological advancement, it is extremely difficult for anyone malicious attacker to gather enough CPU power in outspending the entire network. A feasible attack against a blockchain-based network often needs one body to control over 50 percent of the total CPU power of such a network. The larger the network, the tougher it gets for an attack to be carried out.

However, as already established, the application of blockchain spans beyond simple transactions. Transactions basically go beyond sending assets from one party to another. Actually, this very process can be referred to as a quite simple program: the sender generates a computation (transaction), which can only be carried out if the receiver provides, at some future time, the appropriate inputs. When it comes to the traditional ways of monetary transaction, the appropriate input would be the receiver's proof of ownership. Simply put, a receiver can spend the received coins only if a rightful ownership of those coins can be proven by him or her. Although it sounds a bit unnatural, it is actually not. For example, when performing wire transfers, some sort of credentials or authentication processes are needed to prove the ownership of the account. For some online banking services, this could just be a password and username. At the onsite bank branch, it could be a debit card or some ID card. These processes are often coded into the banking system, however, with blockchain this not necessary.

Note that for Bitcoin transactions, just like bank processes, senders (by deploying a public key to verify identities) can transfer coins to the receiver: this is the traditional "Point A to Point B" monetary transaction, where ID cards are replaced with private and public keys. Nevertheless, this does not stop the further application of blockchain. For instance, timestamped and immutable messages can be stored on the blockchain forever. The older these messages become, the more difficult it is to change them.

While the blockchain concept was conceptualized from cryptocurrency-based research, the blockchain has a vast array of other powerful applications. The job of blockchain is basically to encode a singular factor: state transitions. Once a sender transfers a coin (Bitcoin) to another party, the universal state of the blockchain is altered. For example: account X was holding 100 coins before, but now account X is void and account Y is holding 100 coins. In addition, the blockchain offers a cryptographically safe method of carrying out these state transitions. In simpler terms, any outside party of the transaction can verify the state of the blockchain; likewise, any state transition started by users on the blockchain network can be carried out in a way that is verifiable and secure.

One nice method of explaining blockchain is a never-stopping computation: new data and instructions are tapped from a pool—a pool of unverified transactions. Each result is stored on the blockchain, which creates the computation state. Any single picture of the blockchain is its computational state at that point in time.

In some significant way, every software system works with state transitions. Note that blockchain-based state transitions are not restricted to sending coins.

The decentralized computational feature of blockchain can be applied to several other things. This is where the Ethereum network comes in: a blockchain capable of carrying out any computation as an aspect of a transaction.

Although the landscapes of transactions (between two users) and cryptocurrency are buzzing nowadays when it comes to blockchain, we can actually deploy this technology's secure and distributed computations to other applications.

Moving past Bitcoin: first-generation decentralized apps

While Bitcoin seems to be the standout feature of blockchain, the technology's applications are much more than just being used to spend digital currencies. In reality, there are several hundred ways blockchain technology can be deployed today. In addition, just like email is to the internet, so is Bitcoin to blockchain—a large data store or electronic platform, where applications are built. One of which is currency. Before now, creating blockchain applications demanded an intricate understanding of mathematics, cryptography, coding, and some relevant skills. However, advances have made things easier. Until this time, never-before-imagined applications—such as trading, regulatory compliance, digitally recorded property assets and electronic voting—are now keenly been created and used with greater speed, security and efficiency. Ethereum is opening up new possibilities because it provides developers the tools to create decentralized applications.

Note: a decentralized application is an application executed by several users on a decentralized network. They are created in such a way to circumvent every point of failure. Users, who provide computing power for the execution of this application, are basically rewarded with tokens. Bitcoin, for instance, is an example of a decentralized application because it offers its users peer-to-peer electronic fund system that allows the payment of Bitcoins online. Basically, since decentralized applications consist of code running on a blockchain network, they are not under the control of any central body or individual.

Ethereum—basics

Simply put, Ethereum is a blockchain-based open software platform that allows developers to create and use decentralized applications. Similar to Bitcoin, Ethereum is a blockchain network that is public and distributed. While the two have some substantial distinctions between them, the most vital difference to know is that Ethereum and Bitcoin differ considerably in capability and purpose. Bitcoin provides one specific application of blockchain technology: the peer-to-peer electronic fund system, which permits the payments of Bitcoin. Therefore, while the Bitcoin-based blockchain is deployed in tracking ownership of cryptocurrency (Bitcoins), the Ethereum-based blockchain concentrates on executing the programming code of all decentralized applications.

Since decentralized applications run on the blockchain, Ethereum enjoys the qualities of blockchain. From immutability (third-party entities cannot alter data), to tamper-proof (applications are designed on a consensus network, where censorship is prohibited), to security (securing applications from fraud and cyberattacks, thanks to the usage of cryptography and the absence of any central point of failure), to zero downtime (application cannot be turned off and powered down)

Ether

While Ethereum introduces broad computations to blockchain, it stills deploys "coins." Its coin is referred to as "Ether." In the Ethereum-based blockchain, rather than mining for Bitcoins, miners labor to be rewarded with Ether. Ether is a form of cryptocurrency that powers the Ethereum-based platform. Apart from being used as tokens for transactions, Ether can be deployed by developers (of decentralized application) to pay for transaction services and fees on the Ethereum platform.

"Gas" is the amount token deployed to pay miners who store transactions in blocks; the execution of all smart contracts needs a specific amount of gas to be embedded in it—for the purpose of enticing miners to include such contract in the blockchain.

How smart contracts connect with Ethereum

Ethereum-based blockchain has some amazing abilities. One is that it can be used to create smart contracts—a self-executing contract that handles the execution, administration, performance, and payment associated with the contract. As we already know, a smart contract is computer code that can simplify the exchange of cash, shares, property, intellectual content, or any valuables. Because smart contracts run on the blockchain technology, such contracts work like an autonomous computer program, capable of executing themselves automatically under some certain met conditions. By running on the blockchain, smart contracts execute their programmed instruction with any likelihood of third-party meddling, fraud, downtime, or censorship.

Although all blockchains are capable of processing code, most are highly restricted in their capabilities. Ethereum, however, is significantly wide-ranging in its uses. Instead of granting only a list of restricted operations, Ethereum permits developers to build any operation they desire. In other words, Ethereum-based blockchain can be used in building thousands of application with beneficial uses.

The Ethereum Virtual Machine

Before the conceptualization of Ethereum, the use of blockchain application was very limited to a set of operations. For instance, Bitcoin and other forms of cryptocurrency were designed sole work as a peer-to-peer method of transacting with digital currencies. Soon developers of the blockchain network were facing an issue. To either grow the number of function provided by Bitcoin and other forms of applications, which is severely time-consuming and difficult, or create a new blockchain platform and, as well, a totally new platform. Spotting this issue, Vitalik Buterin—creator of Ethereum—came up with a new method.

The Ethereum Virtual Machine (EVM), a major invention of Ethereum, is Turing-complete software running on the Ethereum network. As long as there are enough computer memory and time, this software lets users run any program, despite the programming language of that program; the EVM permits the seamless and effective building of blockchain applications. Rather than having to create a completely new blockchain for each new application, Ethereum allows the creation of thousands of various applications on a singular platform.

Note that by leveraging Ethereum, any centralized services can become decentralized. Consider each third-party system spread across the various sectors and industries worldwide. From apparent services like bank loans to the less flashy intermediate services involved with regulatory compliance, voting systems, title registries, etc. With centralization gone, ease is raised and the cost of doing business reduced.

Decentralized Autonomous Organizations (DAO)

Ethereum can be deployed to create Decentralized Autonomous Organizations (DAO). A DAO is an organization that is entirely decentralized and autonomous—without one single leader. A DAO is operated by a programming code and run on a collective of smart contracts recorded on the Ethereum-based blockchain. The code is created to substitute the structure and rules of traditional organizations, removing the requirement for centralized authority. The DAO is owned by every party who buy tokens; however, rather than each token representing ownership or equity shares, tokens serve as donations that grant each party voting rights.

A DAO is made up of one or more contracts; in fact, it could be financed by a collective of people who share a goal. Its functions are fully transparent and independent of any human interference, even its original designers. Apart from covering its operating cost, the lifespan of a DAO is dependent on its service usefulness to its customer base.

Shortcomings of decentralized applications

In spite of its numerous benefits, decentralized applications still have their faults. Since smart contract code is basically man-written, smart contracts are only as effective as the person who writes them. Oversights or coded bugs can cause unwanted nefarious actions to take place. Once a code error is exploited, the only way to counter exploitations or attacks is to obtain a network consensus to rewrite the original code. This practice opposes the nature of blockchain that proclaims immutability. Likewise, any action performed by a central body could raise tough questions about an application's decentralized nature.

Using Solidity to Build Ethereum Smart Contract

The process of creating a smart contract requires some simple steps. Your reasons for building one can vary: from understanding how it works to building your dApp (decentralized application) or launching an ICO (Initial Coin Offering).

Note: ICO is a cryptocurrency-based equivalent to an Initial Public Offering (IPO) in the mainstream world of investment.

No matter your intentions, understanding the inner workings of a smart contract is very important. In some years' time, the Ethereum platform has a great potential to create dApps that could alter how we communicate on cyberspace. Although Ethereum uses smart contracts which function as a regular blockchain transaction, such contracts produce a line of condition(s) that needs to be satisfied before an action(s) is carried out. Smart contracts are deployed in multi-signature wallets, blind auctions, crowdfunding, voting, and many other things.

A simple breakdown of the smart contract:

John possesses a steel business in the US, and Matt is his China-based metal supplier. Both men have a wonderful business relationship. Their decade-long relationship is built on trust. Both are enjoying business growth, especially John who sells out steel blocks every time. John then drafts a contract when his steel inventory gets to a specific limit; he automatically makes an order out to Matt for 500 lbs of steel blocks at 50 Ether per ton. Matt approves of this arrangement and takes John's Ether payment immediately. Matt starts supplying to fulfill John's order. Matt can then trade-off his Ether for Yuan at an online exchange website for a small fee and he will cash out instantly. Whether Matt chooses to exchange is Ether or hold on to it is his decision. Whatever his decision, he can instantly reinvest his capital.

Now both men are happy with the arrangement. Customarily, without a smart contract, John has to reach out to his bank and attempt a wire transfer to Matt's Chinese bank. It usually takes about two days for this process to be completed—even so, Matt would endure a waiting time of some days before the bank clears his transfer. Besides, John will be charged a transfer fee by his bank to sending funds to Matt. In such a case, money and time are wasted. As if that is not enough, both men need to battle with the foreign exchange issues, converting US Dollars to Chinese Yuan.

Learning the basics

Note: a little programming knowledge would be useful in this section

To build a smart contract, we must start from scratch. Before we start using a contract, it is crucial to understand the basics. More crucially, the role the Ethereum platform plays in all this.

*Note: if you come across a problem with a program at any point, consider launching the program as administrator. Just right-click it and select **Run as administrator** on your computer.*

Creating an Ethereum node

Basically, an Ethereum node (or client) is a device (software) that can run blockchain—the Ethereum protocol. Though nodes can customarily run on laptops and desktops, mobile platforms are currently being developed. When you run the Ethereum node, you can link up with other nodes on the network, thereby getting straight admission to the blockchain. Hence, we start deploying smart contracts, sending transactions, and mining blocks—all on the blockchain network.

Nodes are written in Python, C++, and Go (Go Ethereum/Geth). In this guide, we will be working with Go—the most widely used of three. Understand that downloading Geth means downloading the complete Ethereum blockchain, which is about 35 Gigabyte of your hard drive's storage.

1. To install Geth, go to the Go Ethereum site to download

2. Then download Geth latest Windows version (as of the publication: version 1.8.7)—ensure it the 64-bit version.

3. After downloading, tap the installer and select I **Agree**.

4. Ensure to check the Geth box and select **Next.**

5. To complete the installation, you will be asked to choose the destination folder. The default folder is: C:\Program Files\Geth.

6. After installation is completed, close the installer.

7. Open a command prompt. For easier input of command lines, you can download a command-line tool like Git Bash; during its installation, ensure to add Git Bash to your PATH variable). Next, type "cd C:\Program Files\Geth" to go to the Geth directory

8. Type "Geth" to initiate synchronization to the Ethereum blockchain. Since this is a first-time synchronization, the whole blockchain from every peer is downloaded. Depending on your internet speed, the download time could take awhile.

After the downloading is done, you can begin to run on your own Ethereum node.

Creating a private Ethereum network

Once getting admission to the Ethereum network through your node, you have to create a personal private server where you can build and use smart contracts. Understand that, for a private Ethereum network, these contracts cannot be used on the Ethereum blockchain, but rather they can be deployed on your own personal blockchain.

Building the first block in your blockchain: (genesis.json)—aka the genesis block

1. Set up a new desktop folder and name it "Private Chain." In this same folder, open a command prompt (press shift + right-click and select **open command window here**) and type "Mkdir chaindata" to set up a data directory subfolder named "**chaindata**."

2. Then, you will have to build and store your genesis.json block in your Private Chain folder. This genesis block will be deployed in initializing your private network and storing data in chaindata—the folder for data directory.

3. Open a notepad on your desktop. Copy the below code, paste it on your notepad, and save the file as "genesis.json" in your Private Chain folder.

```
{
  "coinbase"   : "0x0000000000000000000000000000000000000001",
  "difficulty" : "0x20000",
  "extraData"  : "",
  "gasLimit"   : "0x2fefd8",
  "nonce"      : "0x0000000000000042",
  "mixhash"    :
"0x0000000000000000000000000000000000000000000000000000000000000000",
  "parentHash" :
"0x0000000000000000000000000000000000000000000000000000000000000000",
  "timestamp"  : "0x00",
  "alloc": {},
  "config": {
      "chainId": 15,
      "homesteadBlock": 0,
      "eip155Block": 0,
      "eip158Block": 0
    }
}
```

4. Next, you will have to start up your private network (located in the chaindata directory) by deploying your genesis.json file. Now ask Geth to always put the data directory in the "chaindata" subfolder and also tell Geth where it can find the genesis.json file. Note: ensure genesis.json is never placed in the chaindata subfolder; it is only placed in the Private Chain folder.

To do this, open a command line, type the command below into the command line, which points to the Private Chain folder.

geth --datadir=./chaindata/ init ./genesis.json

5. Ensure that the genesis state was written successfully.

6. Next, start up Geth and link it your personal private chain. Here, the geth.ipc endpoint socket connection and port 30303 opens.

geth --datadir=./chaindata

Anytime Geth is started up, the IPC endpoint opens—this is deployed for processing connections between Geth and programs such as Mist, Ethereum Wallet, and MetaMask. Alternatively, the IPC endpoint is deployed to open the Geth Javascript API console. More of these will be explained as we proceed.

Now, you have created your personal private Geth network.

Meaning of MetaMask

MetaMask functions as an Ethereum wallet as well as a browser. Via MetaMask, one can begin interacting with smart contracts and dApps online without needing to install software or download the blockchain. MetaMask can be used as an extension exclusively on your Chrome browser for depositing Ether or creating a wallet.

Visit this link to download MetaMask.

The Mist browser

Mist can be referred to as an electron application—this means that it is a desktop hybrid application that features a web interface. This feature makes the browser application smoother and faster. Mist is an important and powerful browser because when it launches, a Geth node will run in the background as well, triggering an instant access to the Ethereum-based blockchain network. However, since you are building a smart network, Mist is not needed to access the default Geth node. Instead, you should run your node on your private network.

Ethereum Wallet

Ethereum Wallet is operation in the Mist browser that can exclusively access just one dApp: the wallet app. Written only in Javascript and HTML code and running within the Mist browser, Ethereum Wallet deploys web3.js in managing your accounts. Click here to download the Ethereum Wallet.

1. To download the Mist browser in order to can connect to your own private network, go the Mist page to find the latest version for download.

2. Select **I Agree** after opening up the installer.

3. Select **Next** to choose your default download path: C:\Program Files\Mist (default)

4. Ensure the blockchain data is stored in the default path under **\Roaming\Ethereum**, and then select Install.

Connect Mist your own private network

After setting up your private network with the genesis block, you can set up a command line in your "Private Chain" folder to ask Geth to link up with your datadir. Do so by typing the command into your command prompt:

geth --datadir=./chaindata/

Geth will then begin to run.

Next, open your Mist browser to activate your geth.ipc endpoint. Now the Mist browser will automatically connect to your private network. Ensure Mist is connected by checking if the **Private-Net** sign is visible in the upper-right window of the Mist window. Do not bother with the **Looking for peers** sign since you are on your own network and do not have to link up with other peers.

Fundamentals of the Mist browser

1. On the upper-left corner is the tool bar. Go to the **Develop** tab, under it is the grayed-out Ethereum Node—showing that you are not connected to Geth since you are running your own network. Just like the Chrome browser, you can navigate to the **Developers Tools** beneath the **Develop** tab.

2. On the upper-left side of the Mist browser, like any browser, you can access several open tabs. To open the Ethereum Wallet, click on the green box. This wallet is a distributed application (dApp) that enables your smooth interaction with the Go Ethereum's JavaScript interface.

3. Via https://wallet.ethereum.org/, you are linked up to the Ethereum network. With the Mist browser, you can now watch contracts or deploy contracts, send Ether, as well as view past transactions,

4. Navigate down the Wallets tab, to add new accounts, view your accounts, import or create wallet contracts (such as multi-signature wallet contracts or single owner accounts), and likewise see old transactions.

5. To set up an account, select **Add Account** (which means add wallet), **Create new account**, and then input a strong password. Select **OK** to complete the setup of your wallet.

Beneath the **Send** tab, you can transfer Ether from wallet to wallet or from wallet to contract. After selecting Send, you have a choice of setting the gas (transaction fee). All transactions need some gas level to encourage processing. You can adjust the amount of gas to pay—this depends on how ▢uick you need the transaction sanctioned and processed by the blockchain network.

Now, beneath the **Contracts** tab, you can start watching current contracts and past tokens while deploying new contracts. It is with this tab, you can start creating and deploying your Hello World! contract.

You can likewise watch past tokens and contracts. To interact with a previously used contract, select **Watch Contracts**, input the contract ABI (application binary interface), contract address, and contract name. If you want to watch or spend ERC-20 tokens (Ethereum-generated tokens on the blockchain), enter the token symbol, name, and contract address.

Bonus: Navigate to **the Explorer** tab and click it. This triggers a new web page in the browser. Select connect on the top-right corner to connect with your browser with your wallet—this is a Web 3.0 connection. Now you are able to go to any Ethereum-based distributed applications (dApps) and work with them with your wallet. For instance, you can interact with dApps on sites like this. Since you are on a private network, you can easily connect your wallet your browser. However, you should note that you do not have any Ether yet; therefore, your interaction with these distributed applications will be limited. To enjoy a complete experience, you will have to link up with the Ethereum network and transfer Ether into your wallet. But this does not mean you cannot browse these dApps right now.

The function of Web3.js

Mist is simply a browser, but it is capable of connecting your wallet to a browser and interacting with the Ethereum blockchain. Mist can do all these thanks to a browser injection called Web3.js library; this lets you interact with Ethereum nodes on it while transacting with blockchain-deployed smart contracts.

Keep in mind

While all these may seem too much at first, keep in mind that they will make much sense as you proceed. Now you will have to interact with Remix, use Solidity to write your first smart control, deploy it via Mist, and work with it.

Remix IDE

Remix is a popular, open source tool (also a web browser) used in writing Solidity contracts. Remix IDE (integrated development environment) can likewise be used to test, debug, and deploy smart contracts.

Solidity, on the other hand, is a contract-based programming language that can be used to write smart and implement smart contract on several blockchain platforms.

Now it is down to writing code. Although you can write code straight into the Mist browser, writing your first Solidity code is easier with the Remix IDE. This is because Remix is equipped with some features that give it a more detailed development for beginners starting out with small-sized contracts.

The features of Remix are:

• Integrated debugger (call stack, call data, monitoring variables, and stage by stage instructions)

• Warnings to check for overlapping variable names, constant function, gas cost, and unsafe code.

• Integrated deployment and testing environment.

• Highlights error and syntax.

• Functions with Web3 objects injection.

• Can be deployed straight to Mist or MetaMask

• Static analysis.

To access Remix, visit the official website. In the center of the webpage, you will be able to see the space to enter your code. On the top-left screen corner, you will find some file option for "creating new files", "adding local files, "copying all files to another instance, "connecting to local host," and "publishing open files to anonymous Github Gist."

On the top-left screen corner, you will some tabs you can choose from. Your **Compile** tab helps you in compiling your contract once it is completed (by default: it auto-compiles). When you select **Detail**s, you will see a list of some contracts' details like Web3 deployment code of the contract, ABI, bytecode, and metadata.

The **Support, Analysis, Debugger**, and **Setting**s tabs are all important, so endeavor to familiarize yourself with them. Now, this guide is particularly interested in the Run tab. When you select the Run tab, the contract settings listed below appears:

Environment: You can plug Remix to three forms of environment: Injected Web3, Web3 Provider, and JavaScript VM. Both Injected Web3 and Web3 Provider environments execute only on external tools such as Mist or MetaMask. However, JavaScript VM environment can enable execution both on the Remix browser as well as on the Mist browser.

Account: Remix offers five separate accounts preloaded with Ether (100), which can be utilized when developing your contract

Gas limit: Enter the limit for the amount of gas (transaction feed) linked to your contract.

Gas Price: Enter the amount of gas needed for the processing of the contract.

Value: Enter the amount of Ether linked to the contract.

Going on Solidity

If you have some knowledge of Javascript, you can easily spot its similarities with Solidity. Similar to Javascript, Solidity is a contract-based, high-grade language created to work with the Machine (EVM). It is a statical code written to support intricate user-based types, libraries, inheritance, and many other things.

To create a **Hello World!** contract, set up a state variable named "counter" and give it an initial value of 5. Next, set up a function capable of increasing your state variable by 1, a function capable of decreasing the variable by 1, a function capable of returning your counter, and finally a function capable of destroying the contract.

Your source code version should be the first piece of code to enter into Remix. As of now, the latest version of Solidity compactible with Mist is version 0.4.16. Begin by writing this version as the heading of your contract:

pragma solidity ^0.4.16;

Pragma is a keyword that tells the complier (Remix) how the source code should be treated.

For more on Solidity, visit their website.

States and functions

When broken down to its most basic entities, a smart contract is simply a collection of data (its states) and code (its functions) that tally to a certain blockchain-based contract address.

For instance, the line uint256 counter is used to set up the variable counter of type uint256 (unsigned {meaning exclusively positive—neither positive nor negative} integer of 256 bits). It can then be seen as just one slot in the database, which can be retrieved when you call the code function managing the database. You can even enter a value for the variable counter and also set the types as uint256.

uint256 counter = 5;

Because they are basically function-free, state variables will be used in the first few lines of your contract. After setting your variable counter as uint256 and your value as 5, you can move to the next step.

Next: command a function to increase the value of your counter by 1. To do so, you will have to set up a function and command it to "add" 1 to the counter.

```
function add() public {

  counter++;

}
```

After using the function "add()", your counter will now get a value of 6.

Setting up the contract

To set up your "Hello World!" contract, you must first create a contract named:

```
pragma solidity ^0.4.16;

contract HelloWorld {

}
```

Now, you can introduce the earlier mentioned counter state variable and assign it as an unsigned integer of 256 bit. Then you can set it to a value of 5.

```
pragma solidity ^0.4.16;

contract HelloWorld {

  uint256  counter = 5;

}
```

Now set up two functions under this assigned state variable.

• First function to increase the counter by 1

• Second function to decrease the counter one

```
pragma solidity ^0.4.16;

contract HelloWorld {

 uint256  counter = 5; //state variable we assigned earlier

 function add() public { //increases counter by 1

  counter++;

}

 function subtract() public { //decreases counter by 1

  counter--;

}

}
```

In the above code, both functions are assigned to a modifier named **public**. Because Solidity understands two types of function calls—external calls that create a real Ethereum Virtual

Machine call and internal calls that do not (aka "message call), they are four visibility forms for state and functions variables. Functions are stated as being private, internal, public, or external; public is the set default. Although if you did not include it, Remix will send a warning notification that says that you did not specify your visibility and thereby it will default to public. Still, you should form the habit of always entering your function visibility. This will grand you better understanding of the contract settings as you evaluate your code.

Contingent your called function, you can always alter your state variable. However, you still require a function capable of outputting the value of the counter. To perform this, create a function named "getCounter()" which will be returning the counter. Note that is action is read-only; therefore, tell the function that you want to return a constant. In addition, if you want to return a state variable, tell your function the type you want to return. Here, as previously mentioned, you should return a uint256.

```
pragma solidity ^0.4.16;

contract HelloWorld {

  uint256  counter = 5; //state variable we assigned earlier

function add() public {  //increases counter by 1

  counter++;

}

  function subtract() public { //decreases counter by 1

  counter--;

}

function getCounter() public constant returns (uint256 ) {

  return counter;

  }

}
```

Note: Although when you call functions on the Ethereum, gas is used, however, when you return a constant function, no gas is spent.

Now you have a contact that lets you alter the value of your global variable counter. With this setup, you are capable of increasing your variable counter by 1, decreasing it by 1, and returning it whenever you choose to.

Testing your contract

From here, your code is stored in Remix. Beneath the **Compile** tab, ensure that "Auto-compile" is set default. Navigate to the **Run** tab. Ensure the default settings as set the environment to JavaScript VM, your account has been picked, 3000000 gas limit has been set, and that your gas value and price are set to 0. Beneath the **Run** tab, select "Create." After doing this, you will be able to view the details of your contracts and the three functions you have created in your code:

• "add"

• "subtract"

• "getCounter"

In addition, you can view the state variable in its assigned value of 5. To raise your counter by 1, select "add." To call your recently changed counter, select "getCounter." Hence, you value will be updated to 6. You can as well repeat the process for the "subtract" feature. After all this is done, you have now successfully created your own contract.

Deploy the contract in Mist

After testing and confirming your code in Remit, open Mist (ensure it is linked to the Private Network), consider deploying your code on your private network. Go the Mist's Ethereum Wallet, enter the Contracts tab. Click on "Deploy New Contract", and paste your code from Remix into the source code box. Of course, you need to have Ether in your wallet to proceed. You can mine for Ether on your private network through a miner. This can be done via Geth JavaScript console.

Open a new command prompt window that points to your private network folder (C:/users/name/desktop/private network) and type "geth attach" and press "enter." This action will generate a Geth JavaScript console where you can directly input commands into Geth. To initialize Ether mining, type "miner.start();". Now the console will return to "null," showing that mining has started. Check out your Ethereum Wallet on Mist to see boosts of 5 Ether continually added. To end the miner whenever you want, enter "miner.stop();" in the console.

Note: This self-generated Ether is fake: it can only be deployed in your private Ethereum network and cannot be used to make any transaction on the main Ethereum network.

Now navigate the **Contracts** tab, and then move to "Deploy new contract." Also, ensure your code is in the box allocated for source code. On the right side of that box, select "Hello World." Next, select "DEPLOY" to deploy your contract. You will be prompted to enter your password. Once you have done so, go back to the **Wallets** tab and move down to "Latest Transactions" where you can see your recently deployed contract. You will likewise observe that the contract is showing 0 of 12 confirmations, as it is stagnant in "Creating contract" stage.

This is happening because your contract has not been completed set up, as there no available miners on your network to confirm your recently deployed contract. Begin to mine again via the Geth JavaScript console (miner.start();). After you initiate mining again, the confirmation numbers will begin to rise, ultimately deploying your contract completely.

Next, select the contract name—from here, you can execute contract functions, obtain the contracts interface (ABI), produce a scannable QR code, copy the contract address, and send Ether to the contract.

Your "Hello World" contract will display your "getCounter()" function with the counter state variable of 5. Navigate to "Select function" and choose either to "subtract" or "add" function. Once chosen, click on "execute." Remember you are on a private network so you have to run your own miner to authenticate every transaction. After executing a "subtract" or "add" function, the contract should return a value of 4 or 6 respectively. This shows that you now have a functioning smart contract on your private Ethereum blockchain network capable of interacting with Mist.

Add the self-destruct function

As already established, once a contract is deployed, it is formally included to the Ethereum blockchain; therefore, any part with the contract address is capable of interacting with the contract, to some certain extent. However, what if you, the contract owner, decides to delete it from the blockchain network. Thankfully, Solidity provides a seamless way of ending your contract. This is done by performing a self-destruct operation. Once a contract is self-destructed, all the residual Ether kept in the contract address is transferred to an assigned target and the contract is deleted.

Although you have the option of deleting the contract, you have to ensure that such action can only be carried out by you—the contract creator. It is very dangerous if you do not give self-destruct rights to a specific party.

To begin this process, you need to initially tell your contract who the contract owner is—this is the "msg.sender". Now enter the state variable owner as msg.sender. Since the msg.sender is linked to an address, you have to tell Solidity that the state variable needs to be given an address.

pragma solidity ^0.4.16;

contract HelloWorld {

  uint256 counter = 5; //state variable we assigned earlier

  address owner = msg.sender; //set owner as msg.sender

  ....

}

You can call the self-destruct function "kill". Then set up a provisional statement to make sure the party performing the kill function is, in fact, the creator. To ask the contract to transfer Ether back to contract's owner after self-destruction, "selfdestruct(owner);".

pragma solidity ^0.4.16;

contract HelloWorld {

  uint256 counter = 5; //state variable we assigned earlier

  address owner = msg.sender; //set owner as msg.sender

  function add() public { //increases counter by 1

    counter++;

  }

```
function subtract() public { //decreases counter by 1

counter--;

}

function getCounter() public constant returns (uint256) {

return counter;

}

function kill() public { //self-destruct function,

if(msg.sender == owner) {

selfdestruct(owner);

}

}
```

Now you can return to Mist and recreate a fresh contract with an added ""kill()" function . Note that once a contract is destroyed, its Ether will be transferred to an assigned contract. However, to ensure your contract receives Ether, you must add a function for fallback to its code. Without a fallback option, a contract cannot receive Ether from another self-destructed contract.

To initiate a fallback option, you must have precisely one nameless function in your code. It is this unnamed function you will tag as "payable." To do this, place this function below the ""kill()" function :

```
function () public payable {

}
```

Now your contract can receive Ether from wallets with contract addresses.

The Future of Smart Legal Contracts

Smart contracts are designed to be transparent, accurate, self-governing, and self-sufficient. The potentials and application of a smart contract will make it a powerful tool for executing and performing transactions and legal agreements. However, there are technological and legal challenges that need to be tackled first. Smart contracts (as well smart legal ones) have to be legally enforceable in the court. While many blockchain users believe the law should not play a role smart contract disputes, this is not necessarily true. As long as a transaction is taking place, it is important that smart contracts are made in such a way that they are legally enforced and binding.

In spite of the many benefits of smart contracts, the blockchain technology is still relatively at its infancy, and it would take time for it to become fully mainstream. Therefore, before we embrace this technology, we must be able to clarify its regulatory and legal aspects.

Of course, when it comes to blockchain technology, we are not there yet. We do not yet have a blockchain network with adequate interconnections between financial assets and systems registers. On the basic level, there is a certainty to code. It is a pre-planned assembly of inputs to generate a desired output. Compared with traditional language, it is free from the traps of sub-text and ambiguity.

The certainty of a smart contract is its major advantage. If the code is functioning, there is no room for misunderstanding. Still, many attorneys would argue that, from time to time, intentional ambiguity and the option of qualifying a condition are important tools for a lawyer.

Ethereum is a front-running platform particularly created for smart contracts. While more popular cryptocurrencies, like Bitcoin, is capable of storing and transferring value, Ethereum is able to carry data in arguments forms—this means you can program the platform to perform certain actions once some specific conditions are satisfied. Therefore, you can program a contract to self-execute, as the platform is capable of sending funds once some certain conditions are met.

In theory, if there is sufficient time, the platform will ultimately be capable of solving all computable problems. Nevertheless, realistically, the performance of this platform is contingent upon memory and network speed. While smart contract technology has enjoyed some many advances, the technology is still developing. Before it can be fully adopted into the mainstream, there are usability, centralization risk, and scalability issues that need to be addressed. The scalability issue comes up because the technology depends on network speed. Transactions that are more complex need a much faster network speed, which only a few people have access to.

This could result in centralization risk, as power is majorly available in the hands of a few. Such power concentration could result in a group of malicious bodies conspiring together to authorize fraudulent transactions. Lastly, these so-called smart contracts are still basically write in code and quite readable by the traditional attorney. Special tools will have to be created in bridging this gap of usability.

In the end, as smart contract grows, it will definitely disrupt several sectors. Main sectors like healthcare, manufacturing, real estate, government, and financial services have started testing this innovative technology. Given enough time, complete implementation is bound to occur. Attorneys need to be up to date about how this technology can affect their clients. Transactional attorneys may need to study the technical areas of a smart contract to make sure it is in accordance with the goals and wished of the client. In years to come, litigation lawyers may not have to bother with paper-based contract; instead, they want to know the meaning of the code.

About the Author

"Happiness is not something ready made. It comes from your own actions."

Dennis Roßbach is an Expert in Procurement and a serial entrepreneur in E-Commerce and Blockchain Technology. As a speaker and Advisor he has a wide global network helping companys to grow and prosper. He is an open minded and helpful world traveler. Born 1989 in Germany he finished school and his vocational training. He worked for companys such as Accenture and Rolls-Royce before he founded his first company. The SYBX Group was founded in Germany and has it's headquarter in Luxembourg.

For more details visit www.sybxgroup.lu or get in touch via moien@sybxgroup.lu